NATURAL WONDERS
GIANT'S CAUSEWAY

by Katie Chanez

Ideas for Parents and Teachers

Pogo Books let children practice reading informational text while introducing them to nonfiction features such as headings, labels, sidebars, maps, and diagrams, as well as a table of contents, glossary, and index.

Carefully leveled text with a strong photo match offers early fluent readers the support they need to succeed.

Before Reading

- "Walk" through the book and point out the various nonfiction features. Ask the student what purpose each feature serves.
- Look at the glossary together. Read and discuss the words.

Read the Book

- Have the child read the book independently.
- Invite them to list questions that arise from reading.

After Reading

- Discuss the child's questions. Talk about how they might find answers to those questions.
- Prompt the child to think more. Ask: Did you know about the Giant's Causeway before reading this book? What more would you like to learn about it?

Pogo Books are published by Jump!
5357 Penn Avenue South
Minneapolis, MN 55419
www.jumplibrary.com

Copyright © 2025 Jump!
International copyright reserved in all countries.
No part of this book may be reproduced in any form without written permission from the publisher.

Library of Congress Cataloging-in-Publication Data

Names: Chanez, Katie, author.
Title: Giant's Causeway / Katie Chanez.
Description: Minneapolis, MN: Jump!, Inc., 2025.
Series: Natural wonders | Includes index.
Audience: Ages 7-10
Identifiers: LCCN 2024028552 (print)
LCCN 2024028553 (ebook)
ISBN 9798892135344 (hardcover)
ISBN 9798892135351 (paperback)
ISBN 9798892135368 (ebook)
Subjects: LCSH: Natural monuments–Juvenile literature.
Volcanology–Juvenile literature. | Giant's Causeway (Northern Ireland)–Juvenile literature.
Antrim (Northern Ireland: County)–Juvenile literature.
Classification: LCC QH75 .C425 2025 (print)
LCC QH75 (ebook)
DDC 941.6/15–dc23/eng/20240624
LC record available at https://lccn.loc.gov/2024028552
LC ebook record available at https://lccn.loc.gov/2024028553

Editor: Alyssa Sorenson
Designer: Molly Ballanger

Photo Credits: Krumpelman Photography/Shutterstock, cover; Peter Fuchs/Dreamstime, 1; Luc de Zeeuw/iStock, 3; Giacomo Fatigati/Shutterstock, 4; raclro/iStock, 5; Dawid K Photography/Shutterstock, 6-7; Clare Waddingham/Stockimo/Alamy, 8; Andy J Billington/Shutterstock, 9; Ingrid Pakats/Shutterstock, 10-11; Shutterstock, 12-13; Greg Vaughn/Alamy, 14-15; Krzysztof Nahlik/iStock, 16-17; Peter OToole/Shutterstock, 18; Realimage/Alamy, 19; bnoragitt/iStock, 20-21; Sergei Afanasev/Shutterstock, 23.

Printed in the United States of America at Corporate Graphics in North Mankato, Minnesota.

TABLE OF CONTENTS

CHAPTER 1
Rocky Columns 4

CHAPTER 2
How It Formed 8

CHAPTER 3
Visiting Today 18

QUICK FACTS & TOOLS
At a Glance 22
Glossary 23
Index 24
To Learn More 24

CHAPTER 1

ROCKY COLUMNS

Waves crash against Northern Ireland's shore. It is covered in rocky columns. What is this place? It is the Giant's **Causeway**! The columns stretch nearly four miles (6.4 kilometers) along the northern coast.

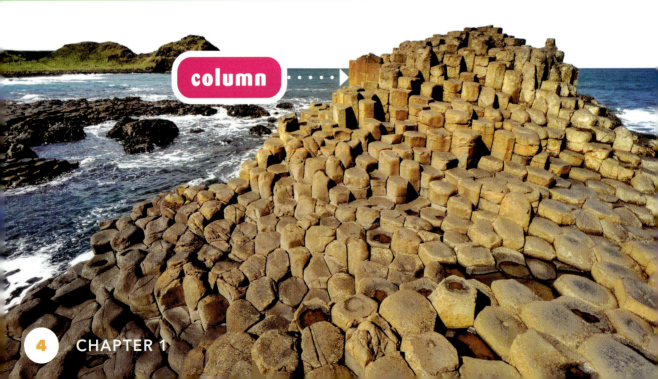

column

There are more than 40,000 rock columns here. Most are hexagon-shaped. They have six sides. Others have five or seven.

hexagon

CHAPTER 1　5

People travel here from around the world. Why? They want to see the unique rocks. They walk along them.

CHAPTER 1   7

CHAPTER 2
HOW IT FORMED

The Causeway's name comes from Irish **folklore**. A giant named Finn McCool is said to have put the rocks here.

Finn McCool

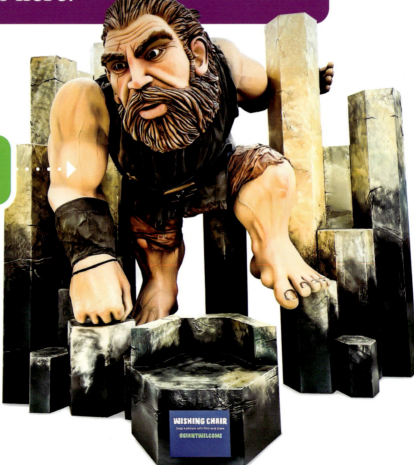

Stories say Finn threw rocks into the water. They formed a bridge from Northern Ireland to Scotland. Why did people think this? There are similar columns at Fingal's Cave in Scotland.

Fingal's Cave

In one story, Finn argued with a very large giant in Scotland. The giant chased Finn back to Northern Ireland. Finn ran so fast his boot fell off! A boot-shaped stone is at the Causeway today. The Scottish giant destroyed the bridge after the chase.

WHAT DO YOU THINK?

The story of Finn is a **legend**. What other legends have you heard? Do you believe them? Why or why not?

CHAPTER 2

Earth is the real cause of the Causeway. Earth is made of **tectonic plates**. About 60 million years ago, the **continents** were close together. Europe was connected to North America. But the plates move.

DID YOU KNOW?

Earth's plates move very slowly. How slow? About 0.6 inches (1.5 centimeters) a year!

As the plates moved, Europe and North America broke apart. **Molten** rock under Earth's **crust** rose to the surface. It formed a **lava** lake where the Causeway is.

DID YOU KNOW?

The Causeway's columns are basalt. This kind of rock often forms columns. Basalt columns can be found all over the world. They are in places like Iceland, Japan, and the United States.

CHAPTER 2   15

Over time, the lava cooled into basalt. As it cooled, the rock cracked. It cracked into columns.

16 CHAPTER 2

TAKE A LOOK!

How did the columns form? Take a look!

1 Tectonic plates pulled apart.

2 Molten rock rose up. It cooled into layers of rock.

3 As the rock cooled, it pulled apart and cracked.

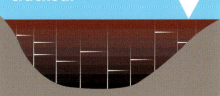

4 Weather and water smoothed the columns.

CHAPTER 2 17

CHAPTER 3
VISITING TODAY

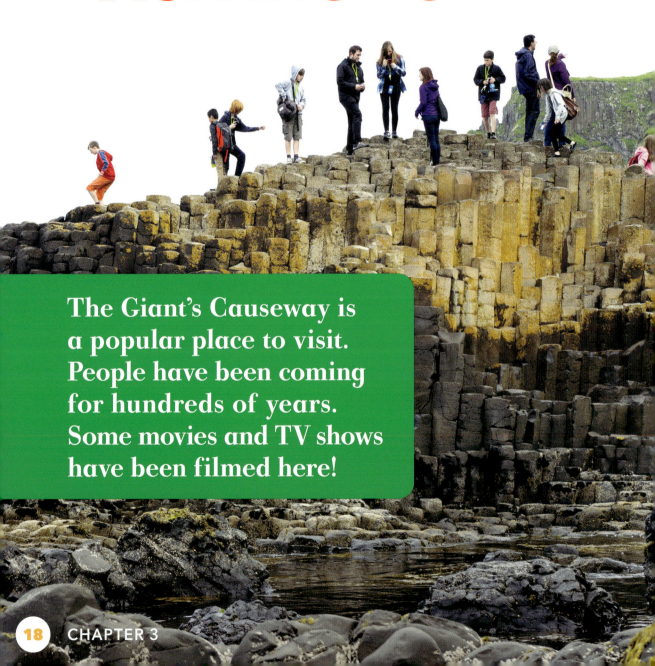

The Giant's Causeway is a popular place to visit. People have been coming for hundreds of years. Some movies and TV shows have been filmed here!

In 2012, a new visitor center opened. It teaches people about the columns. Guides lead people on hikes.

CHAPTER 3

The Giant's Causeway is a **World Heritage Site**. This means it is protected. It is also a **nature reserve**. This keeps the plants and animals that live here safe. This will keep the Causeway beautiful for years to come!

WHAT DO YOU THINK?

Many people travel to see this site. Would you like to visit? Why or why not?

CHAPTER 3

QUICK FACTS & TOOLS

AT A GLANCE

GIANT'S CAUSEWAY

Location:
Northern Ireland

Date Formed:
about 60 to 50 million years ago

How It Formed:
lava cooled into rock and cracked

Number of Yearly Visitors:
about 500,000 people

GLOSSARY

causeway: A raised way across water or wet ground.

continents: The seven large landmasses of Earth including Asia, Africa, Europe, North America, South America, Australia, and Antarctica.

crust: The hard outer layer of Earth.

folklore: A group of people's stories, customs, and beliefs that are handed down from one generation to the next.

lava: Hot, liquid rock that comes out of the earth.

legend: A story that is handed down from earlier times.

molten: Turned to liquid by heat.

nature reserve: An area of land where animals and plants are protected.

tectonic plates: Large, flat sheets of rock that make up Earth's crust.

World Heritage Site: A place with legal protection because it has cultural, historical, or scientific importance.

QUICK FACTS & TOOLS

INDEX

basalt 15, 16
coast 4
columns 4, 5, 9, 15, 16, 17, 19
continents 12
cracked 16, 17
crust 15
Europe 12, 15
Fingal's Cave 9
folklore 8
hikes 19

lava 15, 16
McCool, Finn 8, 9, 11
nature reserve 20
North America 12, 15
Northern Ireland 4, 9, 11
Scotland 9, 11
tectonic plates 12, 15, 17
travel 7, 20
visitor center 19
World Heritage Site 20

TO LEARN MORE

Finding more information is as easy as 1, 2, 3.

① **Go to www.factsurfer.com**
② **Enter "Giant'sCauseway" into the search box.**
③ **Choose your book to see a list of websites.**

24 QUICK FACTS & TOOLS